PARAMEDICS
ON THE SCENE

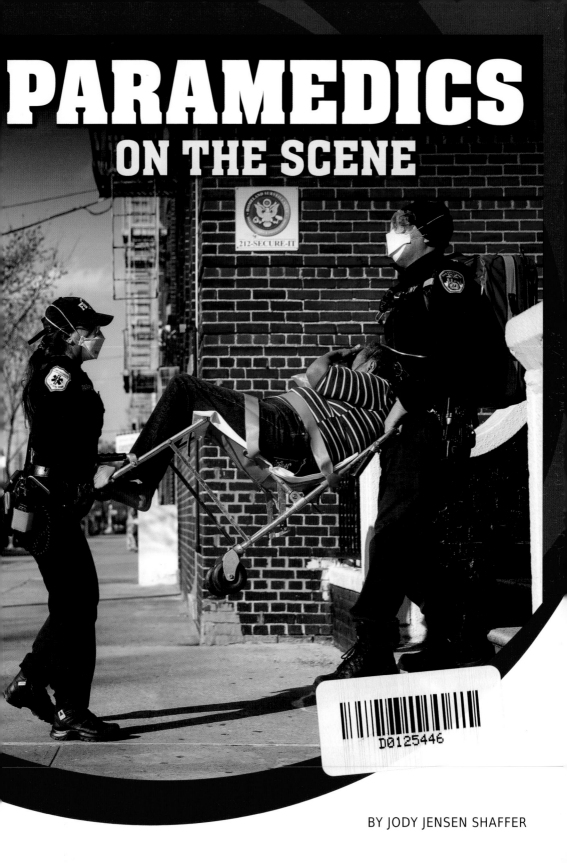

BY JODY JENSEN SHAFFER

Published by The Child's World®
1980 Lookout Drive • Mankato, MN 56003-1705
800-599-READ • www.childsworld.com

Photographs: AP Photo/John Minchillo, cover, 1; Gorodenkoff/Shutterstock.com,
5; LightField Studios, 6, 9; Lopolo/Shutterstock.com, 10; TFoxFoto/Shutterstock
.com, 12; US Coast Guard, 14; Iakov Filimonov/Shutterstock.com, 17; Air Images/
Shutterstock.com, 18; Rawpixel.com/Shutterstock.com, 20

ISBN 9781503855830 (Reinforced Library Binding)
ISBN 9781503856141 (Portable Document Format)
ISBN 9781503856387 (Online Multi-user eBook)
LCCN: 2021940170

Printed in the United States of America

TABLE OF CONTENTS

FAST FACTS

What's the Job?

- Paramedics usually work in emergency rooms and on ambulances. They respond to emergencies. They perform medical services and take patients to hospitals.

- Paramedics must have a high school diploma. They must be certified in **CPR**. Certified means being officially approved to perform a certain skill or job.

- Paramedics must also pass a certification course. All states require paramedics to be licensed.

The Dangers

- The work of paramedics can be physically hard and stressful. The job sometimes involves life-or-death situations. Paramedics may be around people who are upset or scared.

- Paramedics may be around diseases or viruses. Viruses are tiny particles that cause diseases, such as the flu, in people and animals.

- In the United States, the number of work-related injuries and deaths for emergency medical technicians and paramedics is higher than the national average for other occupations.

Important Stats

- In 2019 in the United States, 265,200 people were paramedics.

- There are projected to be 6 percent more paramedic jobs from 2019 to 2029.

- In 2020 the average annual salary for paramedics in the United States was $36,650.

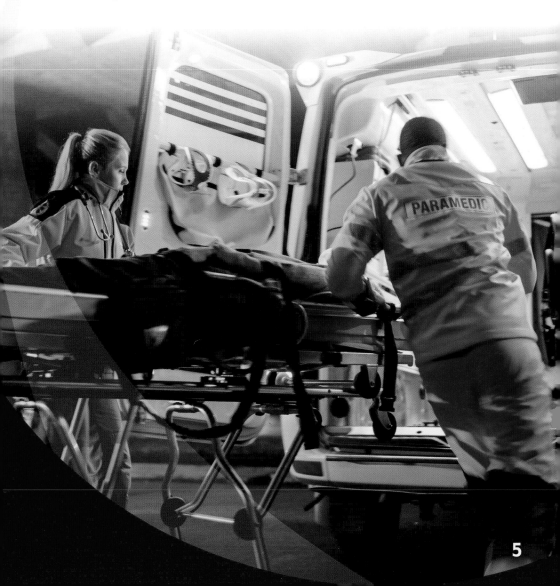

Chapter 1

SHOCK ON THE ICE

Lieutenant Wayne Smith was a firefighter and a paramedic. He was also a hockey coach. But he wasn't supposed to be at the rink at 10:30 p.m. that night. It wasn't his team's night. Wayne had been asked to fill in for a player on another team. So Wayne drove to the rink. He laced up his skates. He was about to hit the ice when he heard someone shout, "Call 911!"

Wayne turned around. He saw a man lying on the ice. Wayne's training took over. He jumped into action. He carefully moved the man off the ice. Then Wayne began CPR. He asked someone to get the rink's **AED** unit. Wayne checked the man for a **pulse**. He didn't feel one. The man's heart was not beating. Wayne knew the man was in cardiac arrest. When a person is in cardiac arrest, their heart stops pumping blood.

◄ **Paramedics begin CPR on a patient whose heart has stopped beating. Paramedics are trained to help in many types of medical emergencies.**

Wayne grabbed the AED. He placed the paddles on the man's chest. Then he shocked the man with electricity. The man's heart didn't start beating. Wayne shocked him again. He waited for a heartbeat. Still, the man's heart was not beating. Wayne tried one more time.

This time he got a heartbeat! Before long, other paramedics arrived. Wayne told them what he'd found. He told them what he'd done. The paramedics took it from there. They put the man on a stretcher. They would continue helping him in the ambulance. The paramedics then rushed him to the hospital.

After his game, Wayne went to the hospital to check on the man. He learned the man had been taken to the heart lab. That was a good sign. The man had made it. For Wayne, it was just another day in the life of a paramedic. But Wayne's actions had meant everything to the man. Wayne's quick thinking and training had saved the man's life.

Paramedics bring patients to the ▶ hospital. They tell doctors what happened to their patients and what medical care they provided.

Chapter 2

HOLDING TIGHT

Scott Rosenfeld was a lifeguard in high school. He was used to watching out for people. He was used to caring for people. But he never thought about doing that as a full-time job. Scott thought he would go to business school. He would wear a suit to work. He would work in an office.

But for now, Scott wanted to earn more money as a summer lifeguard. He could do that by being certified as an **EMT**. He took a class, and he really enjoyed it. Scott decided he didn't want to be a businessman. He wanted to be a paramedic. Scott enrolled in paramedic school. It took a lot of time. He studied hard and got certified. Then he got a job with the Los Angeles Fire Department.

◄ **EMTs and paramedics work together to treat patients and transport them to the hospital quickly and safely.**

▲ **Many firefighters are also EMTs. They are certified to give emergency medical care.**

Scott and his partner had just dropped off a patient at Cedars-Sinai Medical Center. Their radio crackled to life. A woman was having an emergency. She was threatening to jump off the parking garage at the hospital. Scott drove to the roof. He approached the woman slowly. She was sitting near the edge. She didn't want him to come closer.

Scott knew he had to be careful. He didn't want the woman to jump. He put down his medical kit. He sat on it. He talked to the woman. He listened to her. She told him her problems. She didn't think anyone cared.

Scott kept listening. He told the woman she might be feeling sad because of low blood sugar. He wondered if he could check her blood pressure. She said yes. Scott moved in slowly. He placed a blood pressure cuff around her arm. And then he grabbed the woman around her waist. She struggled. But Scott held her back from the edge. Others arrived to help. They pulled Scott and the woman away from the edge. They were both safe. Scott had saved the woman's life.

EMT OR PARAMEDIC?

EMTs and paramedics work together. But they have different jobs. An EMT can give basic emergency medical care. They can calm patients. They can take them to the hospital. EMTs can give people oxygen. They can put on splints to help with broken bones. Paramedics give advanced medical care. They can treat life-threatening illnesses and injuries. They can give medicines. They can start **IV**s. They can read **EKG**s. Paramedics are trained to know if someone is having a heart attack.

Chapter 3

INTO THE RIVER

It was 7:23 a.m. in New York City. Niall O'Shaughnessy and his partner Moses Nelson were sitting in their ambulance at Murray and West Streets. They had already cleaned and restocked their ambulance. Now they were waiting for their first call of the day. Their radio sprang to life. A young woman had jumped into the Hudson River. She was near Pier 25. Niall and Moses turned on their lights and sirens and sped to the scene.

A few minutes later the paramedics hopped out of their vehicle. They saw the woman in the water. She was holding on to a life ring. A Parks Department worker had thrown it to her. But the woman was getting tired. Her grip on the ring was getting loose. The woman let go of the ring. She started to slip under the water. Niall worried that she'd drown. He kicked off his boots. He unclipped his radio. He jumped into the dirty water.

◄ **A Coast Guard rescue boat takes part in a training exercise. Emergency medical workers train often to keep their skills sharp.**

Niall swam to the woman. He spoke to her to keep her calm. "Listen, don't worry. There's going to be a lot of people to help us." He kept her afloat.

Soon a water rescue team from the New York Fire Department sped to the couple. The crew hauled the woman and the paramedic onto their boat. An ambulance rushed the woman to the hospital. She would be OK. Niall was checked out at the scene. He was cold, but he was fine. It was an exciting start to the day for this New York City paramedic.

Paramedics monitor a patient's ▶ heart rate and breathing. Paramedics also comfort their patients while they are treating them.

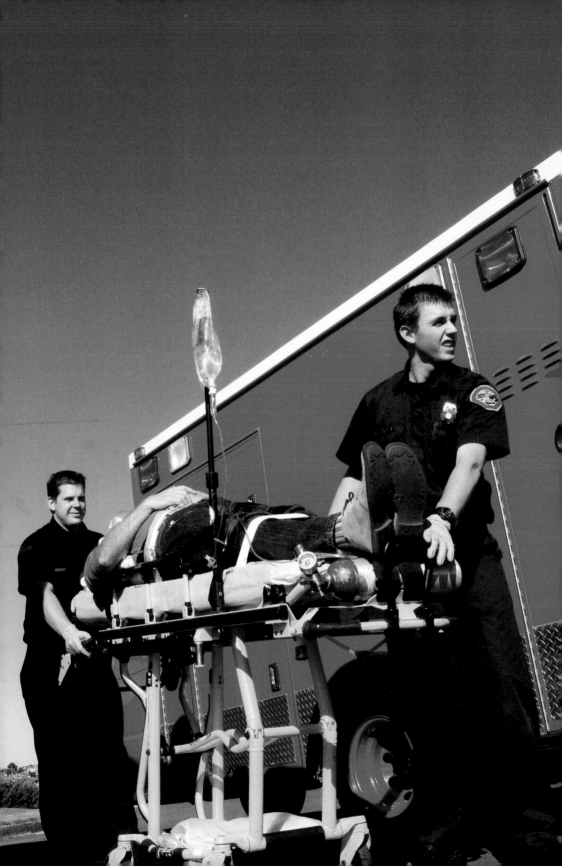

Chapter 4

TRUST YOUR INSTINCTS

Veronica was ice-skating with her boyfriend at the Curry Village ice rink in Yosemite, California. Then she fell and bumped her head. Paramedic Kevin Grange and his partner got the call. They drove to the rink. They wheeled their **gurney** onto the ice. They noticed Veronica was sitting up. She looked a little confused. But she was **conscious**.

Kevin kneeled down. He asked Veronica her name. She told him. Kevin asked where she was now. She said Yosemite. Then he asked the woman what happened. Veronica said she had fallen. She was also able to tell him the name of the president. Kevin decided Veronica was alert and aware.

◀ **Paramedics give medical care on the scene. If more care is needed, they will transport their patient to the hospital.**

▲ Paramedics rely on their training and instincts to determine if a patient's injury is life-threatening and needs urgent treatment.

Veronica's boyfriend said she'd lost consciousness for about 30 seconds. Kevin wondered if she had a **concussion**. It seemed like she would be OK. Then Kevin felt Veronica's pulse. Her heart was beating very fast. Her skin was cool and dry. Kevin and his partner loaded Veronica onto the gurney. They put her in the ambulance.

That's when Kevin started suspecting a different diagnosis. Veronica began saying she was going to get sick. She repeated the phrase over and over. But she didn't get sick. The paramedics tried to calm her. They tried to get her to take slow breaths. All of Veronica's other vital signs were normal. What should they do? Should they release her? Take her to the hospital?

Kevin went with his instincts. He suspected head **trauma**. They needed an air ambulance to fly her to a trauma center. When the helicopter arrived, the paramedics told the flight nurse what had happened. The air crew flew Veronica to the trauma center.

It was a good thing, too. Veronica had a skull **fracture** and bleeding in her brain. She needed emergency surgery. Kevin's quick thinking and good instincts saved Veronica's life.

THINK ABOUT IT

- What do you think are the best and worst parts of being a paramedic?

- What personal characteristics are necessary to be a good paramedic? Why do you think people want to be paramedics?

- Would you like to be a paramedic? Why or why not?

GLOSSARY

AED: AED stands for **a**utomated **e**xternal **d**efibrillator (AH-tuh-may-tud ek-STUR-nul dee-FIH-bruh-lay-tur). It's a device that sends an electric shock to a person's heart to regulate its beat.

concussion (kun-KUSH-un): A concussion is a brain injury caused by a hard blow or collision. Paramedics may check their patients for symptoms of a concussion.

conscious (KON-shus): Being conscious means that you are awake and able to understand what is happening.

CPR: CPR stands for **c**ardio**p**ulmonary **r**esuscitation (KAR-dee-oh-puhl-mu-nair-ee rih-SUH-sih-tay-shun). It is a way to help a person who has stopped breathing.

EKG: EKG is short for electrocardiogram (ih-LEK-troh-KAR-dee-uh-gram). An EKG is a machine that measures and records the heart's electrical activity.

EMT: EMT stands for **e**mergency **m**edical **t**echnician (ih-MUR-jun-see MED-ih-kul tek-NIH-shun). An EMT is a person who provides medical care in an emergency.

fracture (FRAK-chur): A fracture is a break or crack in a bone.

gurney (GUR-nee): A gurney is a hospital bed on wheels that is used to move patients.

IV: IV is short for **i**ntra**v**enous (IN-truh-vee-nuhs). An IV is a device used to let fluids (such as medication or blood) enter a person's body.

pulse (PUHLSS): Pulse is the movement of blood through a person's body that can be felt by touching the person. One step in CPR is checking for a pulse.

trauma (TRAH-muh): A trauma is an injury that is life-threatening. Paramedics are trained to assess and manage traumas.

TO LEARN MORE

Books

Dittmer, Lori. *Amazing Rescue Vehicles: Ambulances*. Mankato, MN: Creative, 2019.

Simon, Samantha. *EMTs and Paramedics*. Philadelphia, PA: Mason Crest, 2018.

Spilsbury, Louise. *Emergency Medical Technician*. New York, NY: PowerKids, 2016.

Websites

Visit our website for links about paramedics:

childsworld.com/links

Note to Parents, Teachers, and Librarians: We routinely verify our Web links to make sure they are safe and active sites. So encourage your readers to check them out!

SELECTED BIBLIOGRAPHY

Chasan, Aliza. "Paramedic Jumps in Hudson River to Save Woman." *New York Daily News*. April 9, 2015. www.nydailynews.com.

Curtiss, Aaron. "Humble Hero Is Named Paramedic of the Year: Award: Scott Rosenfeld's Daring Rescue Saved Woman Threatening to Jump Four Stories to Her Death." *Los Angeles Times*. November 1, 1995. www.latimes.com.

Fire Science Degree Schools. "How to Become a Paramedic: Requirements and Top Training Schools." www.firesciencedegreeschools.com.

Wagner, Jeff. "Trailblazing Female Paramedic Honored for Nearly Half-Century in the Field." WCCO/CBS Minnesota. July 26, 2019. https://minnesota.cbslocal.com.

INDEX

ABOUT THE AUTHOR

Jody Jensen Shaffer is an award-winning poet and the author of more than 80 books of fiction and nonfiction for children. She lives in Missouri with her family.